THE AMAZING VOYAGE OF THE NEW ORLEANS

THE
AMAZING VOYAGE
OF THE NEW ORLEANS

by Judith St. George
drawings by Glen Rounds

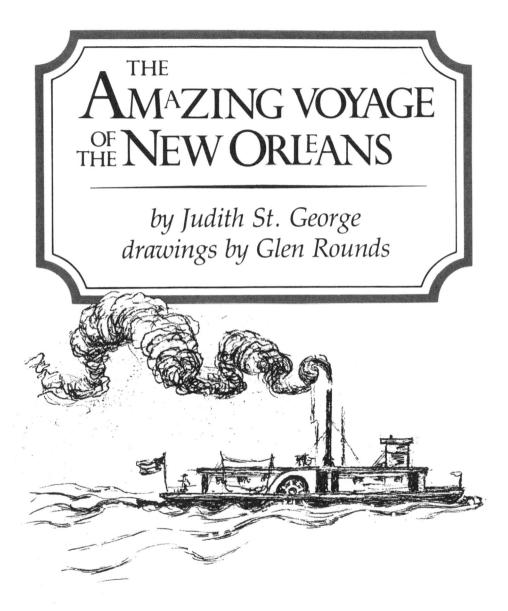

G. P. PUTNAM'S SONS · NEW YORK

Library of Congress Cataloging in Publication Data
St. George, Judith
The amazing voyage of the New Orleans.
Summary: Recounts the voyage in 1811 of the "New Orleans,"
the first steamboat to travel down the Ohio and Mississippi Rivers,
a trip fraught with dangers including
North America's most violent earthquake.
1. Ohio River—Description and travel—Juvenile literature.
2. Mississippi River—Description and travel—Juvenile literature.
3. New Orleans (Steamboat)—Juvenile literature.
4. Roosevelt, Nicholas J., 1767-1854—Juvenile literature.
{1. New Orleans (Steamboat) 2. Steamboats. 3. Roosevelt, Nicholas J.
4. Ohio River—Description and travel.
5. Mississippi River—Description and travel.
6. New Madrid, Mo.—Earthquake, 1811-1812.
7. Earthquakes—Missouri}
I. Rounds, Glen II. Title.
F518.S24   1979   917.7   79-14475
ISBN 0-399-20697-3

With love to Pattie and Lee

INTRODUCTION

No one who lived on the Ohio and Mississippi rivers when this country was young ever forgot the amazing year of 1811. Nature turned topsy-turvy. Though squirrels are not migrating animals, that year thousands and thousands of them migrated south. Many of them drowned trying to cross the wide Ohio River.

On September 17, on a bright and cloudless day, the sun was almost totally eclipsed by the moon. The fall sky held further surprises. The Great Comet of 1811, one of the most spectacular comets of all time, blazed across the night heavens for months. Its head was larger than the sun, over a million miles in diameter. The migrating squirrels, the eclipse and the dazzling comet terrified people who feared they were omens of something terrible to come.

Maybe they were right, for in December the strongest earthquake ever recorded in North America rocked the western waters. Its tremors were felt from upper Canada to the Gulf of Mexico, and from Boston to the Rocky Mountains. It was, in fact, one of the great earthquakes in the history of the world.

Even the weather was strange that fall and winter, warm and sultry.

But that wasn't all that took place on the Ohio and Mississippi rivers in the amazing year of 1811. Perhaps as amazing as the twists and turns of nature was the two-thousand-mile voyage of Nicholas Roosevelt in his steamboat, the *New Orleans*.

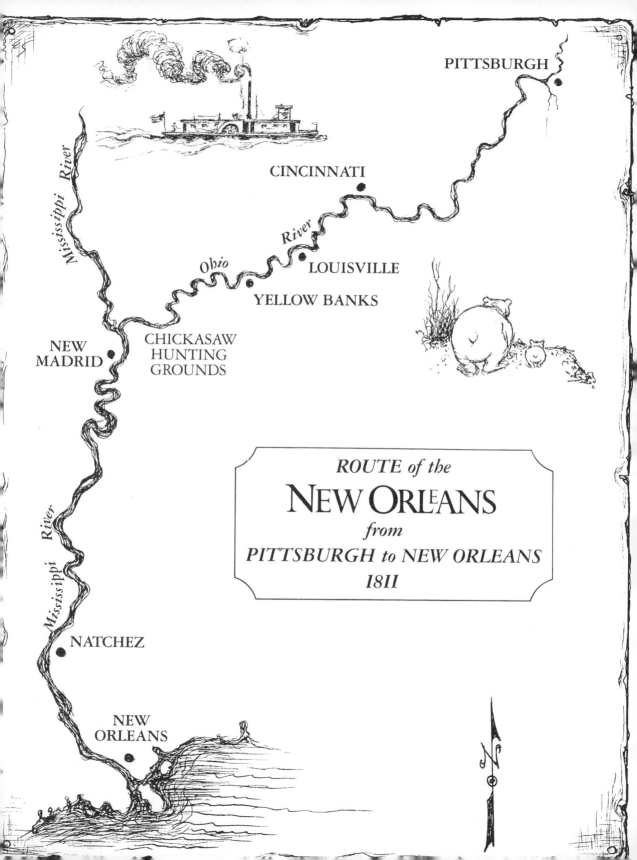

PITTSBURGH

CINCINNATI

Mississippi River

River

Ohio

LOUISVILLE

YELLOW BANKS

NEW
MADRID

CHICKASAW
HUNTING
GROUNDS

Mississippi River

ROUTE *of the*

NEW ORLEANS

from

PITTSBURGH *to* NEW ORLEANS

1811

NATCHEZ

NEW
ORLEANS

One

The clumsy flatboat plunged through the curtain of mist and foam into the rapids of the Ohio River. The bow dipped under the waves, then heaved up, tossing spray over the deck. The passengers held their breath as the roar of the boiling water deafened them. The pilot and the oarsmen muscled the flatboat between huge rock ledges until they reached the channel on the far side of the river. Immediately, the current swept the boat into the chute. She shot down the rock-lined fall. All hands manned the oars to keep her steady in the flume of angry white water. She spun, pitched, then was brought back on course. At last the big flatboat was safely through the two miles of terrible rocks and rapids of the Ohio River known as the Falls of the Ohio.

Nicholas and Lydia Roosevelt were delighted that the most dangerous part of their journey was over. It was July, 1809, and Nicholas and Lydia were on their honeymoon. It wasn't a honeymoon like most honeymoons. No, the Roosevelts were traveling by flatboat from Pittsburgh to New Orleans, two thousand miles down the Ohio and Mississippi rivers.

As soon as their flatboat was in the calm, deep waters below the Falls of the Ohio, Mr. Roosevelt pushed off in his rowboat to measure the river's depth and mark it in his notebook. Mrs. Roosevelt sat on the upper deck under a wide awning. An open book lay in her lap. Sometimes she read while her husband worked. Sometimes she sewed. Today she watched the antics of the colorful river birds.

The five-man crew of the flatboat was used to Mr. Roosevelt's strange ways. He had been measuring the depth of the water and charting the currents ever since they had left Pittsburgh. Mr. Roosevelt had even taken the crew ashore to stockpile coal where they found it along the riverbanks.

None of this seemed strange to Nicholas Roosevelt. It made good sense. He was studying and charting the waters because he planned to build a steamboat and navigate it down the Ohio and Mississippi rivers. The coal would come in handy later for fuel.

In 1809 steamboats only traveled on the eastern rivers. That wasn't good enough for Nicholas Jacobus Roosevelt. He believed that steamboats had a future on the western rivers, too. The few scattered river settlers sent their flour and corn and furs and whiskey down the Ohio and Mississippi rivers by flatboat. But poling their supplies and groceries back up by keelboat took three or four months and was very expensive. These same settlers were so cut off from news of the East, some of them hadn't even heard that Mr. James Madison was the new president of the United States. What a difference in frontier life steamboats would make. They could travel easily down AND up the Ohio and Mississippi rivers, delivering both goods and news.

Two other steamboat men, Robert Fulton and Robert Livingston, dreamed the same dream as Nicholas Roosevelt. The three men became partners. Together they planned to build a steamboat and test it on the western rivers. When the journey was over, the steamboat could carry freight and passengers between Natchez and New Orleans on a regular run.

There was never any question as to who would be in charge. Nicholas Roosevelt would build the steamboat, and Nicholas Roosevelt would take it on its two-thousand-mile journey. But first, the partners decided, Mr. Roosevelt must study and chart the rivers. Good. Nicholas would take his new bride, Lydia, with him. Their flatboat ride down the Ohio and Mississippi rivers would make a dandy honeymoon trip. And it did.

But along the way, Mr. Roosevelt got plenty of advice. When the Roosevelts' flatboat reached Louisville just above the Falls of the Ohio, riverboatmen hooted. "A paddlewheeled steamboat make it over the Falls? Never! Why, those rocks and rapids would break up a deep-hulled steamboat in no time."

Mr. Roosevelt paid them no mind. After he had studied and measured the Falls for three weeks, he was sure a steamboat could safely make it. Watch for me in a year or two, he promised when he left Louisville. I'll be back in my steamboat and show you.

When the Roosevelts reached the Mississippi River, the Mississippi riverboatmen hooted, too. "Maybe a steamboat can

navigate on deep, calm, eastern rivers like the Hudson, but a steamboat can never make it through the terrible currents and snags and floating islands of our great river. You'd be wasting your time and money."

Riverboatmen were big, strapping men. They had to be strong to pole their keelboats up the river against the current. Nicholas Roosevelt was tall and strong, too. More than that, his Dutch determination was very strong indeed. The more the riverboatmen told him it couldn't be done, the more determined he was to do it.

In December, 1809, six months after starting out in Pittsburgh by flatboat, Nicholas and Lydia Roosevelt reached New Orleans. Mr. Roosevelt had listened and watched and studied and measured. Now his mind was made up. He was sure a steamboat could navigate the western rivers and he couldn't wait to start building it.

Two

The following spring, in 1810, Nicholas and Lydia Roosevelt again traveled to Pittsburgh. There, in a shipyard at the Forks of the Ohio, where the Allegheny joins the Monongahela to form the Ohio, Mr. Roosevelt began to build his steamboat. He took charge of every detail. He ordered the finest white oak to be cut from Pennsylvania forests for the ribs and keel, and white pine for the beams and planking. The lumber was rafted down the Monongahela River to the shipyard.

Pittsburgh ship carpenters were the best, but they knew nothing about steam engines. Mr. Roosevelt sent East for mechanics and a shipbuilder. He ordered the huge copper boiler from the East, too. An ox team had to freight it the whole way.

But nothing was too good, or too expensive, for Mr. Roosevelt's steamboat. Finally, after eighteen months, and $38,000, the *New Orleans* was finished.

Mr. Roosevelt's partners back East howled at the terrible cost. Still, all they could do was write angry letters, and angry letters didn't bother Mr. Roosevelt any more than the warnings of doom he heard every day at the shipyard.

On October 20, 1811, the *New Orleans* was ready to start her long journey. Many of the Roosevelts' Pittsburgh friends came down to the shipyard to watch. Mr. Roosevelt was everywhere, running back and forth, making last-minute changes, giving orders to his crew, Pilot Andrew Jack, Engineer Nicholas Baker, the captain, six hands, two maids, a man waiter, and a cook.

Why, there was Lydia Roosevelt boarding the *New Orleans* as well, leading her huge Newfoundland dog, Tiger. The Pittsburghers were astounded. Mrs. Roosevelt was soon expecting a baby. What if the boat blew up or hit a snag and sank? Surely Mr. Roosevelt wasn't going to let his wife risk her life on such a foolish venture.

Mr. Roosevelt was puzzled. Risk? There was no risk. Hadn't he, Nicholas Roosevelt, seen to the design and building of every inch of the *New Orleans?* Of course Mrs. Roosevelt was going.

And of course she did. It was impossible to be married to Nicholas Roosevelt and not have some determination of one's own. After all, Lydia and Nicholas had fallen in love when she was not quite fourteen and he was thirty-six. Though their families and friends disapproved, they had waited four years, then married. Besides, Lydia had done very well, thank you, on their six-month honeymoon trip down the Ohio and Mississippi by flatboat. No, Mrs. Roosevelt was not one to sit home by the fire knitting when she could be on another two-thousand-mile adventure with her husband.

Three

"Whooooot!"

Smoke blew from the tall single smokestack. Slowly the huge paddlewheels began to turn. Slowly the bright blue steamboat edged out into the river. Showman that he was, Mr. Roosevelt knew just what would tickle the fancy of the crowd. He ordered his helmsman to head the *New Orleans* upstream. The helmsman obeyed and the *New Orleans* made a wide circle against the current. Then she turned downstream again and swept past the amazed onlookers.

Hats flew in the air. Ladies waved their handkerchiefs. Though the Pittsburghers wished the Roosevelts all good luck, they were certain the steamboat would never reach New

Orleans. Nicholas and Lydia waved farewell in return. They were just as certain of their success.

Nicholas and Lydia were much too excited to sleep that first night. Together they watched the curve of unbroken forest pass by as they steamed down the majestic Ohio River at ten miles an hour. La Belle Rivière, the French called it, the Beautiful River.

After a week of pleasant traveling, the *New Orleans* cast anchor in the stream opposite Cincinnati. It seemed as if all twenty-six hundred inhabitants had gathered on the riverbank to watch. The Roosevelts had met the people of Cincinnati two years before when they had floated by flatboat down the Ohio River. Mr. Roosevelt had said he would return in a steamboat, but no one had believed him. Now here he was.

"I heard-tell she made near ten miles an hour all the way from Pittsburgh," a man said to his neighbor as he puffed on his long pipe.

"Huh, any flatboat can do that," replied the neighbor. "But mark my words, we shall never, ever see her come back up again, not against the current of the Ohio River."

Nicholas Roosevelt was too busy taking on a supply of coal for fuel to listen. It wouldn't have mattered if he had. Mr. Roosevelt had never paid any mind to what people said about his steamboat, and he wasn't about to begin now. Besides, he was in a hurry. As soon as the coal was aboard, it was full steam ahead.

Two days after leaving Cincinnati, the *New Orleans* dropped anchor opposite the waterfront town of Louisville, Kentucky. It was midnight, and the moon lit up the night as bright as day. The Great Comet of 1811 stretched halfway across the sky, its tail over a hundred million miles long. The engineer released the safety valve. A shriek of escaping steam pierced the quiet.

At the noise, the people of Louisville tumbled from their beds and rushed to the banks of the Ohio River. They were sure that the comet had fallen from the sky, hissing and whistling as it sank in the Ohio River.

What they found was almost as amazing as a comet. A 116-foot-long bright blue steamboat sat at anchor, a ribbon of smoke pouring from her smokestack. And there on the deck to greet them were Mr. and Mrs. Roosevelt and their Newfoundland dog, Tiger.

When the people of Louisville got over their surprise, they gave a public dinner in honor of the Roosevelts. They had grown fond of Nicholas and Lydia two years before when the Roosevelts had spent three weeks in Louisville studying the Falls. Besides, they respected Mr. Roosevelt as a man of his word. He had promised to come back to Louisville in a steamboat, hadn't he? Well, there she was, paddlewheels and all.

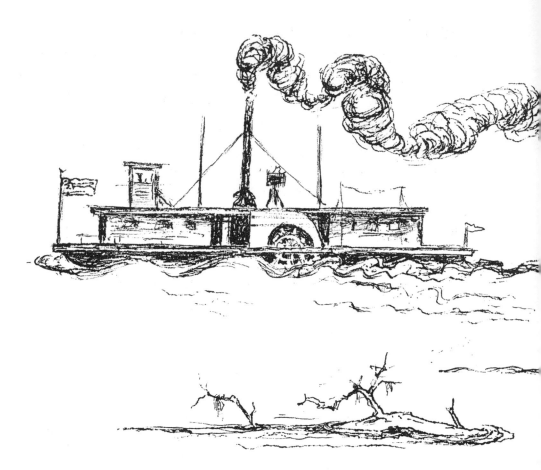

In return, the Roosevelts invited their Louisville hosts to a dinner aboard the *New Orleans*. When everyone was eating and talking and having a good time, machinery began to clank. Deep rumblings sounded underfoot. The *New Orleans* was moving.

The guests jumped to their feet and ran from the dining cabin. They were certain that the anchor cable had broken and the *New Orleans* was drifting downstream toward the Falls of the Ohio, just below Louisville.

No such thing. Mr. Roosevelt had ordered his crew to start the engine. The *New Orleans* wasn't drifting downstream toward the Falls at all. She was chugging along nicely upstream against the current of the Ohio River, with the lights of Louisville disappearing behind her.

The *New Orleans* didn't go far, only a mile or two, but it was far enough. Showman that he was, Mr. Roosevelt had neatly proved to the people of Louisville that his steamboat could go upstream against the current, just as well as down.

Four

As it turned out, the *New Orleans* reached Louisville just in time. Lydia had her baby there on October 30 in the home of a friend. The Roosevelts named their first son Henry Latrobe, after Lydia's family.

Mr. Roosevelt had never been very good at waiting. Like most determined people, when he had something to do, he wanted to do it . . . now. But he had a good long wait in Louisville, more than a month. It was all because the Ohio River was low, too low for the *New Orleans* to pass safely over the two miles of treacherous rocks and rapids of the Falls of the Ohio. Like it or not, Mr. Roosevelt had to wait until the rains fell in the upper country and the river rose. Mrs. Roosevelt was perfectly happy to wait. The extra weeks gave both her and baby Henry time to rest and gain their strength.

Every day Mr. Roosevelt measured the depth of the river. Day after day the river didn't rise. Mr. Roosevelt had to do something to keep busy. What he decided to do was go visiting. He and his crew, without Mrs. Roosevelt this time, boarded the *New Orleans* and steamed back up the Ohio River 141 miles to Cincinnati.

The people of Cincinnati were amazed. They had said good-bye to Mr. Roosevelt a month ago, certain they would never see him again. Now he was back. Mr. Roosevelt graciously took

passengers on short trips up and down the river in his steamboat. Those trips, if nothing else, convinced the people of Cincinnati that the *New Orleans* was more than just a boat driven by a steaming teakettle. For sure, if anyone could take a steamboat all the way to New Orleans, Mr. Roosevelt was the one.

After a few days in Cincinnati, Mr. Roosevelt steamed back to Louisville to wait some more. Louisville was a friendly town of fourteen hundred people with a mile-long waterfront street of tidy brick homes. The townspeople had taken the Roosevelts in like family. The ladies fussed over Lydia and her new baby. That was all well and good, but Mr. Roosevelt had a job to do, and he was in a hurry to do it.

Days passed. Now the crew was as impatient as Mr. Roosevelt, and the December weather didn't help. It was heavy and still, with no air moving. The sun was a red globe in a leaden, cloudless sky. Sometimes it seemed as if a huge wet sheet covered the countryside.

Then, when everyone was about to burst with impatience, the Ohio River began to rise. Day after day, Mr. Roosevelt measured the depth of the river. Finally, after ten days, the river stopped rising. The shallowest part of the Falls of the Ohio was still only five inches deeper than the hull of the *New Orleans.* But Mr. Roosevelt was sure the river would rise no higher. It was now or never. Nicholas Roosevelt, being Nicholas Roosevelt, decided it was now.

Most of the Roosevelts' Louisville friends came to the banks of the Ohio River to say good-bye, and most of them were worried. The *New Orleans* may have gone upstream, even all the way to Cincinnati, but she would never, ever make it safely over the terrible rapids and limestone rock ledges of the Falls of the Ohio.

Mr. Roosevelt would have been happy to leave his wife and new son behind to join him on the far side of the Falls. But every once in a while, Mrs. Roosevelt could be even more determined than her husband. Not only would she go over the Falls of the Ohio in the *New Orleans,* but so would baby Henry Latrobe.

"Full steam ahead!"

If the *New Orleans* were to pass over the Falls, she would have to travel faster than the current, which was very fast indeed. A special Louisville pilot who knew every rock and eddy of the Falls had come aboard. The engineer built up a powerful head of steam. Sparks and pitch and black smoke ribboned from the tall smokestack. The safety valve whistled. The paddlewheels turned faster than they ever had before. The *New Orleans* flew out of sight of the Roosevelts' friends.

Mr. Roosevelt knew when to give orders and when to be still and this was a time to be still. He stood with his wife and son in the stern, Tiger crouched at their feet. The deafening thunder of the rushing water drowned out all sound. The special pilot had to signal to the helmsman with his hands. Black limestone ledges appeared out of the foam. The water whirled and eddied and boiled. Flying spray soaked everyone as all hands braced themselves. The *New Orleans* was going so fast it seemed as if she would pitch forward right into the swirling waters.

After the *New Orleans* was out of sight, the people of Louisville waited for word. They waited so long, they finally decided the *New Orleans* had gone down with everyone on board. Sadly they started toward their homes.

"Ho, there!" It was a young man on horseback riding up the pike. "I jest saw the most amazing sight," he called.

Everyone rushed around him.

"A floating sawmill with a deckful of passengers and a dog as big as a pony jest flew over the Falls of the Ohio. They bounced and bucked and the whole sawmill shook ready to split apart. It was going faster and louder than anything I ever saw."

"Were there any survivors?" the people asked, thinking of the nice Roosevelt couple and their new baby son.

"The whole danged sawmill survived. It's setting right below the Falls, a'steaming and a'puffing. Everyone on board is dancing and shouting for joy. Now don't that beat all?"

Five

Mr. Roosevelt paid the special pilot his two dollars, thanked him and sent him ashore. The *New Orleans* had made it safely over the Falls of the Ohio. The worst was past. The Roosevelts started down the Ohio River with nothing more to bother them than the strange, warm December weather, a heavy, misty sky, rain and thundershowers.

Then, on December 16 at 2 A.M., when the *New Orleans* was anchored near Yellow Banks, Kentucky, a deep rumbling sounded, followed by explosions as loud as the firing of a thousand guns. The steamboat rocked so wildly, everyone on board rushed on deck. It was as if they had been under way, then suddenly grounded.

Earthquake! For the rest of the night, shocks tossed the *New Orleans* around like a cork set to sea. Daylight brought another major shock. Riverbanks slid into the water. The ground rose and fell in earth waves so that the uppermost branches of trees interlocked. Other trees crashed to the ground. Whole islands disappeared. Roarings and hissings and whistlings filled the air. The swells that battered the *New Orleans* were as high as ocean waves. In their rush to escape, flocks of birds darkened the sky.

Nicholas Roosevelt had to make a decision. Should they give up their trip? Should they wait until the earthquakes were over? Mr. Roosevelt didn't know it, and couldn't know it, but that would take almost a year. Or should they keep going? Mr. Roosevelt made up his mind quickly. Earthquake or no earthquake, he was determined to finish what he'd set out to do back in Pittsburgh almost two months before. He had seen to the design and building of the *New Orleans*, hadn't he? An earthquake was the perfect test for a steamboat. If she could make it through an earthquake, she could make it through anything. They started off.

Being under way helped, just as Mr. Roosevelt had hoped it would. Though the jarring of the machinery and the slap-slap of the paddlewheels covered up all but the strongest shocks, poor Tiger felt every tremor. He growled and whined as he paced the deck. When he laid his big head on Mrs. Roosevelt's lap, everyone on board knew the shocks were at their very worst.

Only squatters living along the riverbanks watched the *New Orleans* now. They were superstitious, and terrified at the sight of her. They thought the *New Orleans* was the Devil himself,

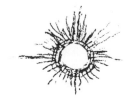

shaking the earth with his great wheels and causing the earthquakes.

As the *New Orleans* made her way from the wide blue-green Ohio into the brown Mississippi, the current slowed. It was a bad sign. The Mississippi must have overflowed its banks. Yes, as the *New Orleans* steamed down the Mississippi past the Chickasaw Hunting Grounds, Mr. Roosevelt saw flooding everywhere. The bottomlands on either shore were underwater. Huge trees were half submerged. The river was foamy and red

41

with mud. Driftwood and broken branches and rubble clogged the waterway.

As the *New Orleans* steamed south, sharp eyes watched. The Chickasaw Indians had already heard of this fearsome creature that was coming down their river. Penelore, they called her, the Fire Canoe. To the Chickasaws, the sparks shooting from the *New Orleans'* smokestack looked like the fiery tail of the Great Comet. The rumble of the engine and the thrashing of the paddlewheels sounded like the rumble of the earthquake. It was an evil omen. The Chickasaws must destroy Penelore before she destroyed them.

Silently, swiftly, the Chickasaws filled their largest cedar-bark war canoe with their bravest warriors. Silently they hid in the half-submerged trees along the flooded shores of their Great

River. Then, as Penelore passed, steaming and shrieking and splashing the water with her big wheels, the war canoe silently and swiftly glided into the water.

"Whoo, whoop, whoop!"

Indians! Nicholas Roosevelt took one look at his pursuers. The *New Orleans* was clearly outnumbered.

"Full steam ahead!"

Side by side, the bright blue steamboat and the slender war canoe raced. Side by side, they both picked up speed. Side by side, until powerful Chickasaw arms began to tire and strong Chickasaw backs grew weary. Steam and paddlewheels won the race. Penelore drew farther and farther ahead until the mists of the Great River swallowed her up from sight of the mighty Chickasaw warriors.

Six

Everyone on board was ready for bed. Earth tremors and an Indian attack had made for a long day. Nicholas and Lydia had just fallen asleep when loud cries and running feet overhead woke them.

Another Indian attack! Mr. Roosevelt was out of bed in an instant. He grabbed the nearest weapon he could find, a slender sword, and raced up on deck. He was ready to do battle, if need be, with the whole Chickasaw nation.

On deck he found an enemy all right, but his sword was useless against it. Fire! Flames and smoke shot from the forward cabin. If something wasn't done, and fast, the whole boat would burn to the water line. A bucket brigade, that's what was needed, and Mr. Roosevelt had seen plenty of those, growing up in New York City. Tossing aside his sword, he put everyone to work. Fill the buckets . . . pass them on . . . throw the water on the flames . . . pass the empty buckets back . . . refill them . . . again and again. . . .

At last the fire was out. The cabin was badly burned, but at least the fire hadn't spread. But how had it started?

One of the crew had stacked green wood close to the stove to dry it, then fallen asleep. The woodpile had caught fire. The dozing hand, half suffocated, had rushed on deck and shouted the alarm.

Earth tremors and an Indian attack in the same day were bad enough. But earth tremors, an Indian attack, AND a fire were altogether too much. Maybe baby Henry Latrobe slept that night, but no one else did, not even Nicholas Roosevelt.

Seven

A day or so later, the *New Orleans* dropped anchor off the little village of New Madrid. The tremors had continued almost hourly, though none were as bad as the two that had hit on December 16. One hundred and forty miles of Mississippi River land had been changed forever. Thousands of acres had sunk twenty-five feet or more. Near New Madrid, the Mississippi River had not only flowed backward, but the river bottom had risen and formed a six-foot waterfall. The waterfall, in turn, had been swept away by the raging currents.

New Madrid was at the very center of the earthquake. Luckily, almost all eight hundred inhabitants survived. But the village itself was practically destroyed. Forever after, that most violent of all North American earthquakes would be called the New Madrid Earthquake.

Some of the people of New Madrid were so frightened at the sight of the fire-belching *New Orleans* they fled inland. Others ran to meet her. But this time the Roosevelts weren't welcomed with cheering or clapping or dinner parties. Fear and panic greeted them.

"Save us. Take us with you," the people begged Mr. Roosevelt.

They didn't care whether the *New Orleans* was a floating sawmill or not. They didn't care if she could travel with the current or against it. All they cared about was escaping the awful shocks that split open the earth in wide cracks and tumbled their waterfront streets into the Mississippi River.

Mr. Roosevelt had to make a decision, and what he decided was painful. He decided not to take anyone on board. There wasn't room for everybody, and supplies were low. There was enough food for family and crew, but not enough for anyone

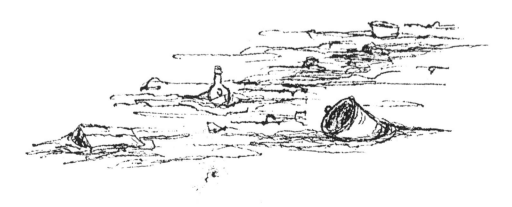

else. Now with the earthquakes, there would be no chance to buy more food until the *New Orleans* reached Natchez, 661 miles to the south. The boat's supply of coal was spent, and wood for fuel was hard to come by. Even if Mr. Roosevelt did let the people come aboard, where would he take them?

Nicholas Roosevelt had one goal right now and that was to reach New Orleans in his steamboat. And he was in a hurry to do it. Did that have a part in his decision? Perhaps . . .

It was time to cast off. The townspeople of New Madrid gathered to watch the *New Orleans* pull up anchor. They were heartsick. Their village was in shambles. Their homes, their church, and even their graveyard were gone. "Take us with you," they begged one last time. "Please take us."

Heartsick themselves, the Roosevelts had to refuse. Farewell, New Madrid, farewell.

Eight

Day after day the tremors continued. Day after day Nicholas Roosevelt kept the *New Orleans* going. Now no one watched her progress at all. The earthquake had destroyed the settlement at Little Prairie. The people of Chickasaw Bluffs had fled into the hills. The trading station at White River was deserted. Walnut Hills was deserted, too. Only an occasional settler came aboard to tell tales of how the earth trembled beneath his feet. The crew already knew that. Their most dreaded task was cutting down trees for fuel each night when the earth trembled beneath their feet the same way.

When the shocks hit during the day, the cracks in the earth

released a purplish gas that darkened the sky. It smelled terrible, like burning brimstone mixed with rotten eggs. When the shocks hit during the night, weird lights flashed low on the horizon.

Sometimes the *New Orleans* steamed past a flatboat or a barge, but there was none of the usual joking back and forth. Only silence passed between them. No one on board felt like talking either. As few orders were given as possible. Silence on board and silence on shore. The millions of beautiful river birds with

their whistling, honking, chirping, squawking, were all gone, flown to safer ground. Only the pesky mosquitoes had stayed, the mosquitoes and the river alligators, whose bellowings and cries and ghostly moans haunted the dark river nights.

The pilot had lost his way. Where he expected to find deep water, he found tree roots and stumps. Islands had changed their shapes. Cutoffs sliced through what was once forest land. Giant trees that had guided riverboatmen for years had disappeared.

At the start of the trip, Mr. Roosevelt had tied up the *New Orleans* to riverbanks each night. No longer. The riverbanks were just as likely to fall into the water as not. Or tall trees fell, smashing everything in their path. Now Mr. Roosevelt tied up the *New Orleans* to trees on the downstream tip of large islands. The island itself protected the boat from driftwood or timber or whatever was floating downstream.

One night, when the *New Orleans* was tied up to an island tree, grating noises and thumpings kept everyone awake.

Bang! Bang! Scritch-scratch. Gurgle . . . glub . . . gurgle . . .

As soon as it was light, Mr. Roosevelt rushed up on deck.

The *New Orleans* must have come adrift in the night. But no, that was the same ancient oak tree on shore that was there last evening. The *New Orleans* hadn't moved. She was still tied up to the island tree, but now the tree was underwater and the island was gone. The night thumpings and jarrings had been drift timber and uprooted trees and clumps of island hitting the *New Orleans* as they broke off and were swept away.

Nicholas Roosevelt was determined to leave, and quickly. Up with the anchor. But the anchor wouldn't budge. It was tangled in the tree branches underwater. Get an ax and cut the anchor cable. That did it.

Full steam ahead!

Nine

At last, at long last, the *New Orleans* left the earth tremors
behind her. The riverbanks no longer slid into the water. Trees
no longer toppled over. Now the pilot sighted familiar
landmarks along the shore. The great swans and ducks and
geese were once again seen winging south down the great
flyway. Bright little parakeets reappeared. Panthers and wolves
and bears once more stalked the dense thickets of cane that grew
along the riverbanks. Here and there settlers again watched Mr.
Roosevelt's amazing mechanical contraption steam by.

The town of Natchez lay ahead. Mr. Roosevelt was in a hurry
to reach Natchez. There he would pick up freight to be
delivered in New Orleans. From then on, carrying freight and

passengers between Natchez and New Orleans would be the steamboat's regular run. Once the *New Orleans* reached Natchez, the long journey was as good as over.

A member of the crew, Nicholas Baker, was in a hurry to reach Natchez as well. He and Mrs. Roosevelt's maid had fallen in love. As soon as they reached Natchez, they planned to be married.

Natchez was a raw, new waterfront town of sixteen hundred people, a mixture of French and Spanish Creoles, Indians, blacks, whites, and free mulattoes. Nicholas and Lydia Roosevelt had visited Natchez on their flatboat trip. Now word of their famous steamboat had reached Natchez before them. On December 30, 1811, crowds gathered on the river bluffs. When the *New Orleans* swung into sight, they began to cheer and clap.

Then the cheering stopped. So did the clapping. The crowds looked at each other in amazement. No smoke blew from the *New Orleans'* smokestack. The paddlewheels were still. The *New Orleans* was drifting downstream, away from the landing. Was this the famous steamboat? Why, she had no more power than a flatboat or a raft.

Like everyone else, the engineer had been looking forward to time off in Natchez, and had gotten careless. He had let the fire get low and the steam pressure had dropped. The *New Orleans* drifted even farther away from the landing.

Nicholas Roosevelt was too much of a showman to put up with that kind of nonsense. Stop the engine. More wood on the fire. Let the steam build up. Finally the paddlewheels bit the water and began to turn. The boat steadied. A few more turns and the *New Orleans* made a little headway. Then, against the current of the great Mississippi River, she swung back toward the landing. The townspeople of Natchez shouted their approval.

Nicholas Roosevelt, with his Dutch determination, had accomplished what he had set out to do, way back in Pittsburgh more than two months before. He had safely brought his amazing steamboat, the *New Orleans,* down the Ohio and Mississippi rivers, overcoming rapids and floods and earthquakes and Indians and fire. He had proved once and for all that steamboats could navigate the western waters. They would never be the same again.

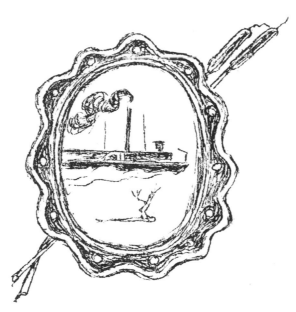

AUTHOR'S NOTE

Nicholas Roosevelt, the great-granduncle of President Theodore Roosevelt, reached New Orleans in his steamboat on January 12, 1812. From then on, the *New Orleans* carried freight and passengers between Natchez and New Orleans until she caught on a snag and sank in 1814. Although she never did go all the way back up the rivers, other steamboats soon made that long journey. By 1817 steamboats were regularly traveling both up and down the Ohio and Mississippi rivers.

Life on the western waters soon changed, just as Nicholas Roosevelt had predicted. Towns and ports sprang up. With a quick, cheap way to get crops to market, farming flourished. Populations multiplied. The settlers' earlier feeling of isolation was gone with the fast distribution of people and goods. Now that their interests were more closely tied to the East, they developed a sense of national identity. The military traveled by steamboat, too, not only in the War of 1812, but also to protect the settlers from Indian uprisings.

What brought improvements to the settlers, brought disaster to the Indians. Increased steamboat traffic saw the end of the Chickasaw way of life forever. Always known as a brave and fiercely independent people, the Chickasaws had to sign over rights to all their lands in 1832. By 1838 the last of the Chickasaws had left their river homeland to live in Oklahoma. To the end, many of them refused to set foot on a "penelore." For the Chickasaw Nation, the *New Orleans* had truly been an evil omen.